"Deeply and impressively subversive, in more ways than one. . . . Kundera's condemnation of modern life is broad, but his sympathy for those who create and suffer it is deep."

—*Time* magazine, on *The Book of Laughter and Forgetting*

"An absolutely dazzling entertainment. . . . Arousing on every level—political, erotic, intellectual, and, above all, humorous."

—*Newsweek*, on *Slowness*

"Audacity, wit, and sheer brilliance."

—*New York Times Book Review*, on *Slowness*

"A novel of possessive passion . . . gets us turning the pages in excitement and alarm, and Kundera's wit keeps us turning them to the very end."

—*San Francisco Chronicle*, on *Identity*

"Erudite and playful. . . . An impassioned account of the émigré as a character on the stage of European history."

—Maureen Howard, *New York Times*, on *Ignorance*

"A voice masterful in its antennae for 'the human condition.' . . . For Milan Kundera, life is plainly elsewhere and where it has always been: in the eye of its fiercely intelligent, endlessly ruminative beholder."

—*Philadelphia Inquirer*, on *Ignorance*

A KIDNAPPED WEST

ALSO BY MILAN KUNDERA

FICTION

The Joke

Laughable Loves

Life Is Elsewhere

Farewell Waltz

The Book of Laughter and Forgetting

The Unbearable Lightness of Being

Immortality

Slowness

Identity

Ignorance

The Festival of Insignificance

ESSAYS

The Art of the Novel

Testaments Betrayed

The Curtain

Encounter

PLAYS

Jacques and His Master

A KIDNAPPED WEST

THE TRAGEDY OF CENTRAL EUROPE

Milan Kundera

Translated from the French by Linda Asher and Edmund White

HARPER

An Imprint of HarperCollins*Publishers*

HarperCollins books may be purchased for educational, business, or sales promotional use. For information, please email the Special Markets Department at SPsales@harpercollins.com.

FIRST EDITION

Library of Congress Cataloging-in-Publication Data has been applied for.

ISBN 978-0-06-327295-8

23 24 25 26 27 LBC 5 4 3 2 1

CONTENTS

THE LITERATURE OF SMALL NATIONS

Presentation by Jacques Rupnik:
"Milan Kundera: Address to the Czech
Writers' Congress, 1967"

Some writers' congresses are more significant, or anyhow more memorable, than the Party's. In Communist Czechoslovakia, these events were frequent and much alike. Writers' conferences could also be unpredictable, and sometimes could even signal profound changes in the relations between the government and the society. Some speeches mark an era, and reading them again today has a special resonance. One such speech is Solzhenitsyn's denunciation of censorship in Moscow in May 1967, which inspired Guy Béart's fine song "La Vérité": "The poet has spoken the truth / He must be executed . . ." Less well known are the startling speeches delivered in Prague a month later at this Writers' Congress, beginning with the one by Milan Kundera.

Kundera was by then a prominent writer—in the theater with *The Keeper of the Keys* (1962); with his story collection *Laughable Loves* (1963, 1965); and above all with *The Joke*, published in 1967 (the year of that congress), a novel that both evoked an era and ended it: a book that remains—for Czech readers but not for Czechs only—linked to the Prague Spring of 1968.* Kundera was teaching at the Prague Film School (FAMU) and had become one of the notable figures in a formidable burst of national cultural creativity. It was a time of exceptional originality and diversity: in literature (Hrabal, Škvorecký, Vaculík), in theater (Havel, Topol), and especially in film (the Czech New Wave with Forman, Menzel, Němec, Chytilová). With good reason, Kundera

---

* The translation of *The Joke* was published in France (Gallimard) the day after the Soviet invasion of Prague in October 1968.

viewed the 1960s as a golden age of Czech culture, which was gradually shedding the ideological constraints of the government without suffering those of the marketplace. From that perspective, the Prague Spring of 1968 cannot be reduced to its political dimension and can only be understood as the culmination of a decade when the writers' magazine *Literární noviny* printed 250,000 copies a week and sold out on the first day; a decade in which the emancipation of the culture was speeding the dissolution of the political structure.

Assessing the danger, the ruling power sought to take back control, and the Writers' Congress of June 1967 became the theater of the struggle between the writers and the regime. The premises of the conflict had been laid earlier, in the 1963 Liblice symposium on Franz Kafka—a symbolic burial of "socialist realism." The work of the Prague (German-speaking) Jewish writer, starting with *The Trial*, reminded Czech readers, forty years later, of another kind of realism, one that was quite disturbing to the current occupant of the Prague Castle—the head of the Communist Party and of the state, Antonín Novotný.

The 1967 Writers' Congress offered a number of

high points: First, in his speech, the writer Pavel Kohout criticized the Soviet Bloc's anti-Israel policy during the Six-Day War and then read out Solzhenitsyn's famous censorship letter. This was too much for Jiří Hendrych, the Party directorate's watchdog for ideological orthodoxy, who abruptly left the room and, as he passed behind the rostrum where Kundera, Procházka, and Lustig were seated, hissed a memorable "That's it, you've lost everything—absolutely everything!" The next day, Ludvík Vaculík—the author of *The Axe* and an editor of *Literární noviny*—took his turn. Seething over Hendrych's exclamation of the day before, he violated all acceptable protocol and raised point-blank the basic issue: the confiscation of power by "a handful of people who want to make all the decisions." He attacked the (Party's) censorship and even the constitution. The break was complete.

Political history will, of course, preserve the explicit details of the writers' conflict with the government: the temporary defeat of the writers in the summer of 1967, then their victory (also temporary) in the spring of 1968. The history of ideas will preserve, especially, Milan

Kundera's opening address. Like his colleagues, he attacks state censorship, but he approaches the theme of creative freedom from another angle. Adopting a historical perspective, Kundera considers the destiny of the Czech nation, whose very existence was not a sure thing, with its elites decimated after the Battle of White Mountain (1620) and then two centuries of Germanization; he returns to the provocative question formulated in the late nineteenth century by the writer Hubert Gordon Schauer: Was it really worth investing such effort to give the Czechs back a language suited to a high culture? Would it not be wiser to blend into German culture, at the time more developed and more influential? Now, nearly a century later, Kundera rhetorically takes up Schauer's question anew and offers his own answer: Such a project would only be justified by an original contribution to European culture and values—that is to say, the universal through the particular. The vitality of the 1960s Czech culture appears to justify that ambition, that gamble. Now that surging culture, critical to the nation's very life, requires freedom to exist. The argument for cultural autonomy and freedom of thought becomes a challenge for the censoring ideologues whom Kundera calls "vandals." Emancipating the culture from the grip of power clearly takes on a political dimension.

But the question Kundera raised in 1967 also carries a startlingly contemporary resonance as he anticipates its further dimension: the fate of the small nations within "the vast integrationist possibilities that have opened up in the second half of the twentieth century." . . . "The process of integration risks absorbing all the small nations, whose only defense can be the vigor of their culture, the personality and the inimitable traits that are their contribution."* Containing the "nonviolent pressure of that integrative process within the twentieth and twenty-first centuries" could turn out far more difficult than was the earlier resistance to Germanization.

Thus the discussion of the particulars of Czech

---

* From a conversation between Milan Kundera and Antonín Liehm in *Trois générations: entretiens sur le phénomène culturel tchécoslovaque* (Three generations: conversations on the Czechoslovak cultural phenomenon). Preface by Jean-Paul Sartre (Paris: Gallimard, 1970). This conversation, which took place on the eve of the 1967 Writers' Congress, may still be Milan Kundera's best intellectual self-portrait.

culture's place continues in Kundera's reflection on the fate of the small Central European nations, and anticipates in some regard their dilemmas in a Europe that is growing ever more global. It is also the link between Kundera's speech to the 1967 Writers' Congress and the essay to appear in 1983 in *Le Débat* on "A Kidnapped West, or The Tragedy of Central Europe."

—Jacques Rupnik

Address to the Czech Writers' Congress:
The Literature of Small Nations

(1967)

My good friends,

Even though since the dawn of time no nation has
lasted forever on the planet Earth, and though the very
notion of "nation" is relatively modern, most take their
own existence for granted—an obvious thing, a gift from
God or from Nature, here perpetually. Their populations
are able to define their culture, their political system,
even their borders as their own creation, and therefore
subject to debate and discussion, whereas their existence
as a people they see as a given, exempt from any debate.
But the troubled and disjointed history of the Czech
nation, which has moved through the antechamber of
death, has allowed the Czechs to avoid falling into that

sort of misleading illusion; the existence of the Czech nation has never been experienced as taken for granted, obvious, and that very uncertainty is one of its major attributes.

This phenomenon was most flagrant early in the nineteenth century, at a time when a handful of intellectuals tried to resuscitate first Czech, that nearly forgotten language, and then a generation later the already half-extinct Czech people. That renewal was a deliberate act and, like any act, it rested on a choice between "for" and "against." Even those inclined toward the "for," the intellectuals coming from the movement for Czech National Revival, recognized the weight of the other side. They knew—for instance, Matouš Klácel discussed it—that a "Germanization" would have simplified life for the Czechs, offering their children wider opportunities. They knew, too, that belonging to a larger nation confers a greater weight to any work of the intellect, and broadens its significance, whereas science articulated in the Czech language—here I quote Klácel himself—"circumscribes recognition of my assiduous work." They were aware of the difficulties that would face the modest peoples who, as Jan Kollar said, "only think and feel halfway" and whose level of education—I quote Kollar again—"is often mediocre and feeble; not living, merely surviving, they neither grow nor thrive, only vegetate; put forth not trees but only weeds."

A thorough awareness of these arguments as well as of the counterarguments places the question of "to be or not to be, and why?" at the very foundations of the modern existence of the Czech nation. That the protagonists of the national awakening favored that existence posed a great challenge for the future: They set for the people the task of justifying, forever, the correctness of their choice.

It was utterly within the logic of that "non-obviousness" of the Czech nation's existence that in 1886 Hubert Gordon Schauer threw a scandalous question into the face of the young Czech society already starting to slump into its smallness: "Would we not have brought more to humankind if we had joined our creative energy to that of a larger nation whose culture is markedly more developed than the Czech culture, just new growth, as it is? All our efforts to revive our people—were they worth it? Is the cultural value of our people great enough to justify its existence? And another question: Will that value in itself be enough to arm it in the future against the risk of losing its own sovereignty?"

The Czech provincialism that was content to vegetate rather than to live saw Schauer's query—substituting doubt for false certainties—as an attack on the nation, and for that reason decided to exclude Mr. Schauer from the project. Nonetheless, five years later, the young critic F. X. Salda declared Mr. Schauer the greatest figure of his time and his essay a patriotic act par excellence. He was not wrong. Schauer had only pressed to its extreme a dilemma familiar to all the leaders of the Czech National Revival. František Palacký wrote: "If we do not lift the nation's spirit upward to greater, nobler activities than those our neighbors undertake, we shall not manage to guarantee even our own existence." And Jan Neruda went further: "We must raise up our nation to the world's level of consciousness and education, if we are to ensure not only its prestige but its very survival."

The leaders of the Czech Revival linked the nation's survival to the cultural values that the nation should produce. They hoped to measure those values not in terms of their usefulness to the nation but rather by criteria—as was said at the time—relevant to the whole human race. They aspired to bring together the world and Europe. In that context, I would underscore a specific feature of Czech literature that has produced a model fairly rare elsewhere in the world: that of the translator as a major, if not the principal, literary actor. Overall, the greatest literary personages of the century preceding the White Mountain debacle* were translators: Řehoř Hrubý of Jelení, Daniel Adam of Veleslavín, Jan Blahoslav. The celebrated translation of Milton by Josef Jungmann established the fundamentals of the Czech language in the era of National Renewal: Czech literary translation is still considered among the world's finest, and the translator commands the same esteem as any other literary figure. The reason for the major role played by literary translation is obvious: it is thanks to translations that Czech established and honed itself as a full-fledged European

---

* The Battle of White Mountain (November 8, 1620) was one of the first and most important battles of the Thirty Years' War; it marked the end of Czech independence.

language, European terminology included. Indeed, it is by way of literary translation that the Czechs founded their own European literature in the Czech language, and that that literature created European readers who read Czech.

For large European nations with what is termed a classical tradition, the European framework in which they evolved goes unremarked. But Czechs, having alternated periods of waking and slumber, have missed several important phases of development of a European mentality, and have time and again had to adapt to its cultural framework, to take possession of it, and reconstruct it. For Czechs, nothing has ever constituted an indisputable possession—neither their language nor their belonging to Europe. This means a perpetual choice between two options: either let the Czech language wither till it is reduced to a mere European dialect—and Czech culture to mere folklore—or else become a European nation with all that that involves.

Only that second option guarantees a real existence—but an existence often quite harsh for a society which, through the entire nineteenth century, devoted most of its energy to building its basic elements, from establishing secondary education to constructing an encyclopedia.

And yet, from the start of the twentieth century and especially between the two wars, we have witnessed a cultural surge unequaled in all of Czech history. Through two decades, a whole pleiad of brilliant minds devoted their genius to creation, and within that very brief period succeeded for the first time since Comenius in hoisting Czech culture to the European level while preserving its own particular features.

That major period—so brief and so intense that we still feel nostalgic for it—was more like adolescence than adulthood: only just beginning, Czech literature was mainly lyrical in character, and to develop what it needed most was a long, uninterrupted peacetime. Breaching so fragile a culture—first by the Nazi occupation and then by Stalinism—for nearly a quarter century, isolating it from the rest of the world, trimming back its many internal traditions, reducing it to the rank of simple propaganda—that was a tragedy that risked relegating the Czech nation once again, this time definitively, to the cultural periphery of Europe. If, over these past several years, Czech culture has caught its breath again, if it has now undoubtedly become the major arena of our success, if a good number of fine works have been created and certain arts—for instance, Czech cinema—are living their golden age, then we are witnessing the most extraordinary phenomenon of Czech life in recent years.

But is our national community properly aware of all this? Does it realize that it could reconnect with that memorable time—the adolescence of our literature, between the wars—and that the idea presents a fine opportunity for the nation? Does it see that the community's own destiny depends on that culture's? Or have people come to disavow the view of the leaders of the Czech Revival that, without strong cultural values, the survival of a people as such is far from guaranteed?

Since the Czech National Revival, the role of culture in our society has doubtless changed, and today we no longer risk falling under an oppression that is ethnic in nature. Still, I do believe that the culture is as important as ever to justify and preserve our national identity. Vast integrationist perspectives have opened up over the second half of the twentieth century. For the first time, humanity has joined efforts to bring about a common history. Small entities are coming together to form larger ones. International cultural collaboration grows tighter. Tourism has become a mass phenomenon. Consequently, the role of several major world languages grows more significant and, as all of life becomes more international, the weight of the smaller languages steadily shrinks. A short while ago, I was chatting with a theater worker, a Flemish Belgian. He was lamenting that his language is under threat—that the Flemish intelligentsia are becoming bilingual, starting to prefer English to their mother tongue, as it facilitates contact with international science. In such circumstances, smaller peoples can protect their language and their sovereignty only through the cultural weight of their language itself—and the singular character of the values engendered and preserved through its help. Of course, the beer made here in Pilsen is such a value, yes. Still, people everywhere drink it as "Pilsner Urquell." No, the term "Pilsner beer" cannot support the Czech claim to their own living language into the future; the endlessly globalizing world will go on asking us, bluntly and quite legitimately, to justify that national existence we chose to resurrect a hundred fifty years ago and will interrogate us on the *why* of that choice.

It is crucial that the whole of Czech society become fully aware of the essential role played by its culture and its literature. Czech literature—this is its other particularity—is scarcely aristocratic; it is a plebeian literature tightly bound to its broad national audience. This is both its strength and its weakness: The strength lies in its solid populist base, where the spoken word resonates so powerfully; its weakness lies in its limited range, in the level of education, in its broad manner, and in the occasional marks of a coarseness in the Czech society it reflects so closely. . . .

At times I fear that our present-day education could lose that European character so important to our humanists and to the leaders of the Czech National Revival. Greco-Roman antiquity and Christianity—those two fundamental sources of the European mind, which provoke the tension for its own development—those elements have nearly vanished from the consciousness of a young Czech intellectual: an irrecoverable loss. But there does exist a solid continuity in European thought that has persisted through all the intellectual revolutions, thought that has built out its vocabulary, its terminology, its allegories, its myths, as well as its favored causes—without mastery of which, European intellectuals could not understand one another. I have just read a devastating report on what future teachers of Czech know about European literature, and I prefer not to hear about their command of world history. Provincialism is not only a feature of our literary outlook; it is above all a problem of the society as a whole—its education, its journalism, and so on.

I recently saw a film called *Daisies*, which tells the story of two marvelously ignorant young ladies, thoroughly proud of their charming narrow-mindedness, who merrily destroy whatever lies beyond their own understanding. I felt I was watching an allegory of vandalism— with broad significance and scorching immediacy.

Who is a vandal? It is absolutely not the illiterate peasant who in a fit of fury sets fire to the rich landowner's mansion. The vandals I myself run into are all of them educated, pleased with themselves, socially well situated, and not especially resentful toward anyone. The vandal, rather, is that prideful narrow mind, pleased with itself and ever ready to claim its rights. That proud narrow-minded fellow believes that the power to fit the world to his own image is among his inalienable rights and, since the world is largely made up of matters beyond his capacities, he adapts the world to his image by destroying it. Thus, an adolescent knocks the head off some statue in a park because the statue infuriatingly seems a better human than he; and since any act of self-affirmation brings man satisfaction, he does it with delight. Men who live only their own contextless present, who know nothing of the historical continuity around it and who lack culture, can transform their nation into a desert with no history, no memory, no echoes, and untouched by beauty.

Vandalism in our time comes not only in forms condemned by the law. When a committee of citizens or bureaucrats managing a project decrees that some statue (or château, or church, or age-old linden tree) is useless and must be eliminated, that is just another form of vandalism. There is no great difference between legal and illegal destruction, just as there is none between destruction and prohibition. A member of Parliament recently demanded, in the name of twenty-one deputies, the banning of two major Czech films, both difficult—one of them (what an irony!) that "allegory of vandalism," *Daisies*. Unabashed, he attacked the two films readily admitting—his exact words—that he hadn't understood them. The illogic of his complaint only seems obvious. The worst crime he charged to the two cinematic works is just that—by surpassing their judges' capacities, the works had offended them.

In a letter to Helvetius, Voltaire wrote this magnificent line: "I do not agree with what you say but I will defend to the death your right to say it." Here you have the articulation of the basic ethical principle of our modern culture. He who regresses into history before the birth of that one principle thereby abandons the Enlightenment and returns to the Middle Ages. Any repression of an opinion, even the brutal repression of wrong opinions, essentially goes against the truth—that truth that is found only by setting free and equal opinions one against the other. Any interference in freedoms of thought and of expression—whatever the means or the title of that censorship—is, in the twentieth century, a scandal as well as a heavy burden for our effervescent young literature.

One thing is incontestable: If today our arts are thriving, it is thanks to the advances in freedom of thought. The fate of Czech literature is now closely related to the extent of that freedom. I know that no sooner do we say "freedom" than someone gets agitated and starts to protest that the freedom of a socialist literature must have its limits. It is clear that any freedom has its limits, which are determined by the state of knowledge, the breadth of prejudice, the level of education, and so on. Still, no new progressive era was ever defined by its own limits! The Renaissance did not define itself by the narrow naïveté of its rationalism—that quality became visible only after the fact—but rather by a rationalist liberation from the earlier boundaries. Romanticism did define itself, by moving beyond classicist canons and by the new material it could perceive once it had crossed the old frontiers. Similarly, the term *socialist literature* will not take on a favorable meaning until it has accomplished that same liberating breakthrough.

In this country, though, we continue to see greater virtue in defending frontiers than in crossing them. Various political and societal situations act to justify a number of restrictions to freedom of thought. But a politic worthy of the name is one that privileges substantive interests over immediate ones. And, for the Czech people, the greatness of their culture is surely that substantive interest.

This is even more true now that Czech culture has fine prospects before it in these times. In the nineteenth century, the Czech people lived at the margins of world history; over the course of the current century, we stand at its center. A life at the center of history is not—this we know—a bowl of roses. Still, on the magical terrain of the arts, torments can turn into creative richness. On that terrain, even the bitter experience of Stalinism can become an asset, as great as it is paradoxical. I don't like it when people put fascism and communism on an equal footing. Fascism, based on a straightforward antihumanism, created a relatively simple situation in moral terms: having presented itself as the antithesis of humanist principles and virtues, it left them intact. By contrast, Stalinism took over the legacy of a great humanist movement that, despite the Stalinist fury, has managed to retain a good number of the original postures, ideas, terms, and dreams. To see that humanist movement turn into its opposite, carrying with it the whole of human goodness, transforming the love of mankind into cruelty toward man, love of truth into denunciation, and so forth—this forces an unexpected vision of the very fundaments of human values and virtues. What is history, what is man's place in history—what is man himself, finally? You cannot answer all these questions the same way before and after that experience. No one emerges from it as the same person he was on entering.

Of course, Stalinism alone was not the sole cause. The peregrinations of the Czech people through democracy, the fascist yoke, Stalinism, and socialism (a history made harsher by a very complicated ethnic environment) have reproduced all the major elements of twentieth-century history. It may allow us Czechs to ask more pertinent questions, and to create myths more meaningful than those of peoples who have not made the same journey.

Throughout this century, our people has doubtless

lived more ordeals than many others, and if its genius has lain silent, it may by now know more. That greater experience could evolve into a liberating breakthrough of the old frontiers, a surpassing of the current limits of man's knowledge and of his destiny, and thereby give Czech culture a meaning, a greatness, and a maturity. For the moment, this is probably only a possibility—mere potentiality; still, a number of works created in these recent years do attest to the reality of such an opportunity.

However, I must wonder once again: Is our national community aware of this possibility? Does it know it owns it? Does it know that such a historic opportunity doesn't come twice? Does it know that to waste such an opportunity would mean ruining the twentieth century for the Czech people?

"It is commonly agreed," Palacký wrote, "that the Czech writers allowed our nation to avert her death, woke her to life, and set out noble aims for her efforts." And in our own time as well it is the Czech writers who bear a major responsibility for the answer to the question of the very survival of our people: it will depend on the quality of Czech literature, on its greatness or its smallness, its courage or its cowardice, its provincialism or its universality.

But is this survival worth the trouble? Is the survival of its language itself also worth it? These essential questions, which were laid down within the foundation of the nation's modern existence, still await definitive answers. So whoever might—through bigotry, vandalism, lack of culture, or narrow-mindedness—obstruct the cultural wheels accelerating now would be obstructing the [wheels of the] very existence of this people.

—Translated from the French by Linda Asher (the French translation of the Czech original was the work of Martin Daneš)

A KIDNAPPED WEST

A Kidnapped West, or
The Tragedy of Central Europe, 1983

MILAN KUNDERA
Presentation by Pierre Nora

Appearing in *Le Débat* in November 1983 (no. 27), this
article, instantly translated into most European languages,
had an impact disproportionate to its brevity. Twenty
pages that, in the East, set off a tidal wave of reaction,
discussion, and polemic from Germany and Russia, and
that in the West—in Jacques Rupnik's words—"reshaped
the mental map of [pre-1989] Europe." What was so ex-
plosive about those pages?

At a time when the West no longer saw Central Eu-
rope as anything more than a part of the Eastern Bloc,
Kundera vehemently reminded the West that Central
Europe, by its culture, belonged entirely to the West and

that, in the case of those "small nations" uneasy about their historical and political existence (Poland, Hungary, Czechoslovakia), culture had always been and still remained the sanctuary of their identity.

Kundera, whose own personal formation was powerfully affected by the revival of the arts, of literature, and of the cinema in 1960s Czechoslovakia, saw that cultural vitality as an element in preparing the Prague Spring: a culture that was not a privileged invention of the elites but rather the living value around which the people itself gathered. He extended his consideration to the cultural heritage of all Central Europe, with Hungary's "grandiose" revolt in 1956 and the Polish uprisings of 1956, 1968, and 1976. "Central Europe: the maximum of diversity in the minimum of space."

The drama of Central Europe is doubled by that of the West, which does not care to see it, has never even noticed its disappearance; which does not register its significance, because the West no longer understands itself, either, in its own cultural role. In the Middle Ages, Europe's unity rested on Christianity; then in modern times, on the Enlightenment. But these days that coherence is replaced by a culture of entertainment, bound up with markets and information technologies. So what meaning can we assign to the European project?

The value of this present text comes not only from its expressive power but from the author's so very personal, anguished voice—which in our time sounds as the voice of one of Europe's greatest writers.

"A Kidnapped West" played a decisive role in the formation of French intellectuals such as Alain Finkielkraut, in his defense of "small nations" during the Yugoslav Wars; in his book *The Defeat of the Mind* in 1987; and, that same year, in the establishment of his magazine *Le Messager européen* [The European Messenger]. More insidiously, Kundera's essay prepared minds for the enlargement of Europe to the Eastern countries. Who knows if its diffuse influence is not still active in the determination of some Central European countries to stay loyal to their own historical heritage and their cultural heritage?

—Pierre Nora

The Tragedy of Central Europe

(1983)

1.

In November 1956, the director of the Hungarian News Agency, shortly before his office was flattened by artillery fire, sent a telex to the entire world with a desperate message announcing that the Russian attack against Budapest had begun. The dispatch ended with these words: "We are going to die for Hungary and for Europe."

What did this sentence mean? It certainly meant that the Russian tanks were endangering Hungary and with it Europe itself. But in what sense was Europe in danger? Were the Russian tanks about to push past the Hungarian borders and into the West? No. The director of the Hungarian News Agency meant that the Russians, in attacking

Hungary, were attacking Europe itself. He was ready to die so that Hungary might remain Hungary and European.

Even if the sense of the sentence seems clear, it continues to intrigue us. Actually, in France, and in America, one is accustomed to thinking that what was at stake during the invasion was neither Hungary nor Europe but a political regime. One would never have said that Hungary as such had been threatened; still less would one ever understand why a Hungarian, faced with his own death, addressed Europe. When Solzhenitsyn denounces communist oppression, does he invoke Europe as a fundamental value worth dying for?

No. "To die for one's country *and* for Europe"—that is a phrase that could not be thought in Moscow and Leningrad; it is precisely the phrase that could be thought in Budapest or Warsaw.

2.

In fact, what does Europe mean to a Hungarian, a Czech, a Pole? For a thousand years their nations have belonged to the part of Europe rooted in Roman Christianity. They have participated in every period of its history. For them, the word *Europe* does not represent a phenomenon of geography but a spiritual notion synonymous with the word *West.* The moment Hungary is no longer European—that is, no longer Western—it is driven from its own destiny, beyond its own history: it loses the essence of its identity.

"Geographic Europe" (extending from the Atlantic to the Ural Mountains) was always divided into two halves that evolved separately: one tied to ancient Rome and the Catholic Church, the other anchored in Byzantium and the Orthodox Church. After 1945, the border between the two Europes shifted several hundred kilometers to the west, and several nations that had always considered themselves Western woke up to discover that they were now in the East.*

---

* The responsibility of Central European Communists who, after the war, did so much to set up totalitarian regimes in their countries is enormous. But they would never have succeeded without the initiative, the violent pressure, and the international power of Russia. Just after the victory, Central European Communists understood that not they but the USSR was the master of their countries; from that point began the slow decomposition of Central European regimes and parties.

As a result, three fundamental situations developed in Europe after the war: that of Western Europe, that of Eastern Europe, and, most complicated, that of the part of Europe situated geographically in the center— culturally in the West and politically in the East.

The contradictions of the Europe that I call Central help us understand why during the last thirty-five years the drama of Europe has been concentrated there: the great Hungarian revolt in 1956 and the bloody massacre that followed; the Prague Spring and the occupation of Czechoslovakia in 1968; the Polish revolts of 1956, 1968, 1970, and of recent years. In dramatic content and historical impact, nothing that has occurred in "geographic Europe," in the West or the East, can be compared to the succession of revolts in Central Europe. Every single one was supported by almost the entire population. And, in every case, each regime could not have defended itself for more than three hours if it had not been backed by Russia. That said, we can no longer consider what took place in Prague or Warsaw in its essence a drama of

Eastern Europe, of the Soviet Bloc, of communism; it is a drama of the West—a West that, kidnapped, displaced, and brainwashed, nevertheless insists on defending its identity.

The identity of a people and of a civilization is reflected and concentrated in what has been created by the mind—in what is known as "culture." If this identity is threatened with extinction, cultural life grows correspondingly more intense, more important, until culture itself becomes the living value around which all people rally. That is why, in each of the revolts in Central Europe, the collective cultural memory and the contemporary creative effort assumed roles so great and so decisive—far greater and far more decisive than they have been in any other European mass revolt.*

---

* For the outside observer, this paradox is hard to understand; the period after 1945 is at once the most tragic for Central Europe and also one of the greatest in its cultural history. Whether written in exile (Gombrowicz, Miłosz), or taking the form of clandestine creative activity (in Czechoslovakia after 1968), or tolerated by the authorities under the pressure of public opinion—no matter under which of these circumstances—the films, the novels, the plays, and the works of philosophy born in Central Europe during this period often reach the summits of European culture.

It was Hungarian writers, in a group named after the Romantic poet Sándor Petöfi, who undertook the powerful critique that led the way to the explosion of 1956. It was the theater, the films, the literature, and the philosophy that, in the years before 1968, led ultimately to the emancipation of the Prague Spring. And it was the banning of a play by Adam Mickiewicz, the greatest Polish Romantic poet, that triggered the famous revolt of Polish students in 1968. This happy marriage of culture and life, of creative achievement and popular participation, has marked the revolts of Central Europe with an inimitable beauty that will always cast a spell over those who lived through those times.

3.

One could say, we'll admit that Central European countries are defending their threatened identity, but their situation is not unique. Russia is in a similar situation. It, too, is about to lose its identity. In fact, it's not Russia but communism that deprives nations of their essence, and that, moreover, made the Russian people its first victim. True, the Russian language is suffocating the languages of the other nations in the Soviet empire, but it's not because the Russians themselves want to "Russianize" the others; it's because the Soviet bureaucracy—deeply a-national, antinational, supranational—needs a tool to unify its state.

I understand the logic. I also understand the predicament of the Russians who fear that their beloved homeland will be confused with detested communism.

But it is also necessary to understand the Pole, whose homeland, except for a brief period between the two world wars, has been subjugated by Russia for two centuries and has been, throughout, subject to a "Russianization"—the pressure to conform to being Russian—as patient as he has been implacable.

In Central Europe, the eastern border of the West, everyone has always been particularly sensitive to the dangers of Russian might. And it's not just the Poles. František Palacký, the great historian and the figure most representative of Czech politics in the nineteenth

century, wrote in 1848 a famous letter to the revolutionary parliament of Frankfurt in which he justified the
continued existence of the Hapsburg Empire as the only
possible rampart against Russia, against "this power
which, having already reached an enormous size today,
is now augmenting its force beyond the reach of any
Western country." Palacký warned of Russia's imperial
ambitions; it aspired to become a "universal monarchy,"
which means it sought world domination. "A Russian
universal monarchy," Palacký wrote, "would be an immense and indescribable disaster, an immeasurable and
limitless disaster."

Central Europe, according to Palacký, ought to be a family of equal nations, each of which—treating the others
with mutual respect and secure in the protection of a
strong, unified state—would also cultivate its own indi-
viduality. And this dream, although never fully realized,
would remain powerful and influential. Central Europe
longed to be a condensed version of Europe made up

of nations conceived according to one rule: the greatest variety within the smallest space. How could Central Europe not be horrified facing a Russia founded on the opposite principle: the smallest variety within the greatest space?

Indeed, nothing could be more foreign to Central Europe and its passion for variety than Russia: uniform, standardizing, centralizing, determined to transform every nation of its empire (the Ukrainians, the Belarusians, the Armenians, the Latvians, the Lithuanians, and others) into a single Russian people (or, as is more commonly expressed in this age of generalized verbal mystification, into a "single Soviet people").*

And so, again: Is communism the negation of Russian history or its fulfillment?

Certainly it is both its negation (the negation, for example, of its religiosity) *and* its fulfillment (the

---

* One of the great European nations (there are nearly forty million Ukrainians) is slowly disappearing. And this enormous, almost unbelievable event is occurring without the world realizing it.

fulfillment of its centralizing tendencies and its imperial dreams).

Seen from within Russia, this first aspect—the aspect of its discontinuity—is more striking. From the point of view of the enslaved countries, the second aspect—that of its continuity—is felt more powerfully.

4.

But am I being too absolute in contrasting Russia and Western civilization? Isn't Europe, though divided into east and west, still a single entity anchored in ancient Greece and Judeo-Christian thought?

Of course. Moreover, during the entire nineteenth century, Russia, attracted to Europe, drew closer to it. And the fascination was reciprocated. Rilke claimed that Russia was his spiritual homeland, and no one has escaped the impact of the great Russian novels, which remain an integral part of the common European cultural legacy.

Yes, all this is true; the cultural betrothal between the

two Europes remains a great and unforgettable memory.* But it is no less true that Russian communism vigorously reawakened Russia's old anti-Western obsessions and turned it brutally against Europe.

But Russia isn't my subject and I don't want to wander into its immense complexities, about which I'm not especially knowledgeable. I want simply to make this point once more: on the eastern border of the West—more than anywhere else—Russia is seen not just as one more European power but as a singular civilization, an *other* civilization.

In his book *Native Realm*, Czesław Miłosz speaks of the phenomenon: in the sixteenth and seventeenth centuries, the Poles waged war against the Russians "along distant borders. No one was especially interested in the

---

* The most beautiful union between Russia and the West is the work of Stravinsky, which summarizes the whole thousand-year history of Western music and at the same time remains in its musical imagination deeply Russian. Another excellent marriage was celebrated in Central Europe in two magnificent operas of that great Russophile, Leoš Janáček: one of them based on Ostrovski (*Katya Kabanova*, 1921), and the other, which I admire immensely, based on Dostoyevsky (*From the House of the Dead*, 1928). But it is symptomatic that not only have these operas never been staged in Russia but their very existence is unknown there. Communist Russia repudiates misalliances with the West.

Russians. . . . It was this experience, when the Poles found only a big void to the east, that engendered the Polish concept of a Russia situated 'out there'—outside the world."*

Kazimierz Brandys, in his *Warsaw Diary*, recalls the interesting story of a Polish writer's meeting with the Russian poet Anna Akhmatova. The Pole was complaining: his works—all of them—had been banned.

She interrupted: "Have you been imprisoned?"

"No."

"Have you at least been expelled from the Writers' Union?"

"No."

"Then what exactly are you complaining about?" Akhmatova was genuinely puzzled.

Brandys observes: "Those are typical Russian consolations. Nothing seems horrible to them, compared with the fate of Russia. But these consolations make no sense to us. The fate of Russia is not part of our con-

---

* Czesław Miłosz's books *The Captive Mind* (1953) and *Native Realm* (1959) are basic: the first close analyses that are not Manichaean toward Russian communism and its *Drang nach West*.

sciousness; it's foreign to us; we're not responsible for it. It weighs on us, but it's not our heritage. That was also my response to Russian literature. It scared me. Even today I'm still horrified by certain stories by Gogol and by everything Saltykov-Shchedrin wrote. I would have preferred not to have known their world, not to have known it even existed."

Brandys's remarks on Gogol do not, of course, deny the value of his work as art; rather they express the horror of the world his art evokes. It is a world that— provided we are removed from it—fascinates and attracts us; the moment it closes around us, though, it reveals its terrifying foreignness. I don't know if it is worse than ours, but I do know it is different: Russia knows another (greater) dimension of disaster, another image of space (a space so immense that entire nations are swallowed up in it), another sense of time (slow and patient), another way of laughing, living, and dying.

This is why the countries in Central Europe feel that the change in their destiny that occurred after 1945 is not merely a political catastrophe, it is also an attack on their civilization. The deep meaning of their resistance is the struggle to preserve their identity—or, to put it another way, to preserve their Westernness.*

5.

There are no longer any illusions about the regimes of Russia's satellite countries. But what we forget is their essential tragedy: these countries have vanished from the map of the West.

Why has this disappearance remained invisible? We can locate the cause in Central Europe itself.

The history of the Poles, the Czechs, the Slovaks, the Hungarians has been turbulent and fragmented. Their traditions of statehood have been weaker and less con-

---

* The word *central* contains a danger: it evokes the idea of a bridge between Russia and the West. T. G. Masaryk, the founding president of Czechoslovakia, had already spoken of this idea by 1895: "It's often said that Czechs have as our mission to serve as a mediator between the West and the East. This idea is meaningless. The Czechs are not next to the East (they are surrounded by Germans and Poles, that is, the West), but also there is no need whatsoever for a mediator. The Russians have always had much closer and more direct contacts with the Germans and the French than with us, and everything the Western nations have learned about the Russians they have learned directly, without mediators."

tinuous than those of the larger European nations. Boxed in by the Germans on one side and the Russians on the other, the nations of Central Europe have used up their strength in the struggle to survive and to preserve their languages. Since they have never been entirely integrated into the consciousness of Europe, they have remained the least-known and the most fragile part of the West— hidden, even further, by the curtain of their strange and scarcely accessible languages.

The Austrian Empire had the great opportunity of making Central Europe into a strong, unified state. But the Austrians, alas, were divided between arrogant pan-German nationalism and their own Central European mission. They did not succeed in building a federation of equal nations, and their failure has been the misfortune of the whole of Europe. Dissatisfied, the other nations of Central Europe blew apart their empire of 1918, without realizing that, in spite of its inadequacies, it was irreplaceable. After the First World War, Central Europe was therefore transformed into a region of small, weak states, whose vulnerability ensured first Hitler's conquest and ultimately Stalin's triumph. Perhaps for this reason, in the European memory, these countries always seem to be the source of dangerous trouble.

And, to be frank, I feel that the error made by Central Europe was owing to what I call the "ideology of the Slavic world." I say "ideology" advisedly, for it is only a piece of political mystification invented in the nineteenth century. The Czechs (in spite of the severe warnings of their most respected leaders) loved to brandish naively their "Slavic ideology" as a defense against German aggressiveness. The Russians, on the other hand, enjoyed making use of it to justify their own imperial ambitions. "The Russians like to label everything Russian as Slavic, so that later they can label everything Slavic as "Russian," the great Czech writer Karl Havlíček declared in 1844, trying to warn his compatriots against their silly and ignorant enthusiasm for Russia. It was ignorant because the Czechs, for a thousand years, have never had any direct contact with Russia. In spite of their linguistic kinship, the Czechs and the Russians have never shared a common *world*: neither a common history nor a common culture. The relationship between the Poles and the Russians, though, has never been anything less than a struggle of life and death.

Joseph Conrad was always irritated by the label "Slavic soul" that people loved to slap on him and his books because of his Polish origins, and about sixty years ago he wrote that "nothing could be more alien to what is called in the literary world the 'Slavic spirit' than the Polish temperament with its chivalric devotion to moral constraints and its exaggerated respect for individual rights." (How well I understand him! I, too, know of nothing more ridiculous than this cult of obscure depths, this noisy and empty sentimentality of the "Slavic soul" that is attributed to me from time to time!)*

---

* There is an amusing little book named *How to Be an Alien* in which the author, in a chapter titled "Soul and Understatement," speaks of the Slavic soul: "The worst kind of soul is the great Slav soul. People who suffer from it are usually very deep thinkers. They may say things like this: 'Sometimes I am so merry and sometimes I am so sad. Can you explain why?' (You cannot, do not try.) Or they may say: 'I am so mysterious . . . I sometimes wish I were somewhere else than where I am.' Or 'When I am alone in a forest at night and jump from one tree to another, I often think that life is so strange.'" Who would dare to make fun of the great Slavic soul? Of course the author is George Mikes, of Hungarian origin. Only in Central Europe does the Slavic soul appear ridiculous.

Nevertheless, the idea of a Slavic world is a commonplace of world historiography. The division of Europe after 1945—which united this supposed Slavic world (including the poor Hungarians and Romanians, whose language is not, of course, Slavic—but why bother over trifles?)—has therefore seemed almost like a natural solution.

6.

So is it the fault of Central Europe that the West hasn't even noticed its disappearance?

Not entirely. At the beginning of our century, Central Europe was, despite its political weakness, a great cultural center, perhaps the greatest. And, admittedly, while the importance of Vienna, the city of Freud and Mahler, is readily acknowledged today, its importance and originality make little sense unless they are seen against the background of the other countries and cities that together participated in, and contributed creatively to, the culture of Central Europe. If the school of Schönberg founded the twelve-tone system, then the Hungarian Béla Bartók, one of the greatest musicians of the twentieth century, knew how to discover the last original possibility in music based on the tonal principle. With the work of Kafka and Hašek, Prague created the great counterpart in the novel to the work of the Viennese Musil and Broch. The cultural dynamism of the non-German-speaking countries was even further intensified after 1918, when Prague offered the world the innovations of structuralism and the Prague Linguistic Circle.* And in Poland the great trinity of Witold Gombrowicz, Bruno Schulz, and Stanisław Witkiewicz anticipated the

---

* Structuralist thinking started toward the end of the 1920s in the Prague Linguistic Circle. It was made up of Czech, Russian, German, and Polish scholars. During the 1930s, in this very cosmopolitan environment, Mukařovský worked out his structuralist aesthetics. Prague structuralism was organically rooted in Czech formalism of the nineteenth century. (Formalist tendencies were stronger in Central Europe than elsewhere, in my opinion, thanks to the dominant position of music, and, therefore, of musicology, which is "formalist" by its very nature.) Inspired by recent developments in Russian formalism, Mukařovský went beyond its one-sided nature. The structuralists were the allies of Prague avant-garde poets and painters (thereby anticipating a similar alliance that was created in France thirty years later). Through their influence, the structuralists protected avant-garde art against the narrowly ideological interpretation that has dogged modern art everywhere.

European modernism of the 1950s, notably the so-called theater of the absurd.

A question arises: Was this entire creative explosion just a coincidence of geography? Or was it rooted in a long tradition, a shared past? Or, to put it another way: Does Central Europe constitute a true cultural configuration with its own history? And if such a configuration exists, can it be defined geographically? What are its borders?

It would be senseless to try to draw its borders exactly. Central Europe is not a state: it is a culture or a fate. Its borders are imaginary and must be drawn and redrawn with each new historical situation.

For example, by the middle of the fourteenth century, Charles University in Prague had already brought together intellectuals (professors and students) who were Czech, Austrian, Bavarian, Saxon, Polish, Lithuanian, Hungarian, and Romanian with the germ of the idea of a multinational community in which each nation would have the right to its own language: indeed, it was under the indirect influence of this university (at which the religious reformer Jan Hus was once rector) that the first Hungarian and Romanian translations of the Bible were undertaken.

Other situations followed: the Hussite revolution; the Hungarian Renaissance during the time of Matthias Corvinus, with its international influence; the advent of the Hapsburg Empire as the union of three independent states—Bohemia, Hungary, and Austria; the wars against the Turks; the Counter-Reformation of the seventeenth century. At this time, the specific nature of Central European culture appeared suddenly in an extraordinary explosion of baroque art, a phenomenon that unified this vast region, from Salzburg to Vilnius. On the map of Europe, baroque Central Europe (characterized by the predominance of the irrational and the dominant position of the visual arts and especially of music) became the opposite pole of classical France (characterized by the predominance of the rational and the dominant position of literature and philosophy). It is in the baroque period that one finds the origins of the extraordinary development of Central European music, which from Haydn to Schönberg, from Liszt to Bartók, condensed within itself the evolution of all European music.

In the nineteenth century, the national struggles (of the Poles, the Hungarians, the Czechs, the Slovaks, the Croats, the Slovenes, the Romanians, the Jews) brought into opposition nations—insulated, egotistic, closed off—that had nevertheless lived through the same great existential experience: the experience of a nation that chooses between its existence and its nonexistence; or, to put it another way, between retaining its authentic national life and being assimilated into a larger nation. Not even the Austrians, though belonging to the dominant nation of the empire, avoided the necessity of facing this choice: they had to choose between their Austrian identity and being submerged by the larger German one. Nor could the Jews escape this question. By refusing assimilation, Zionism, also born in Central Europe, chose the same path as the other Central European nations.

The twentieth century has witnessed other situations: the collapse of the Austrian Empire, Russian annexation, and the long period of Central European revolts, which are only immense bets staked on an unknown solution.

Central Europe therefore cannot be defined and determined by political frontiers (which are inauthentic, always imposed by invasions, conquests, and occupations), but by the great common situations that reassemble peoples, regroup them in ever new ways along the imaginary and ever-changing boundaries that mark a realm inhabited by the same memories, the same problems and conflicts, the same common tradition.

7.

Sigmund Freud's parents came from Poland, but young Sigmund spent his childhood in Moravia, in present-day Czechoslovakia. Edmund Husserl and Gustav Mahler also spent their childhoods there. The Viennese novelist Joseph Roth had his roots in Poland. The great Czech poet Julius Zeyer was born in Prague to a German-speaking family; it was his own choice to become Czech. The mother tongue of Hermann Kafka, on the other hand, was Czech, while his son Franz took up German. The key figure in the Hungarian Revolution of 1956, the writer Tibor Déry, came from a German-Hungarian family, and my dear friend Danilo Kiš, the excellent novelist, is Hungarian-Yugoslav. What a tangle of national destinies among even the most representative figures of each country!

And all the names I've just mentioned are those of Jews. Indeed, no other part of the world has been so deeply marked by the influence of Jewish genius. Aliens everywhere and everywhere at home, lifted above national quarrels, the Jews in the twentieth century were the principal cosmopolitan, integrating element in Central Europe: they were its intellectual cement, a condensed version of its spirit, creators of its spiritual unity. That's why I love the Jewish heritage and cling to it with as much passion and nostalgia as though it were my own.

Another thing that makes the Jewish people so precious to me: in their destiny, that fate of Central Europe seems to be concentrated, reflected, and to have found its symbolic image. What is Central Europe? An uncertain zone of small nations between Russia and Germany. I underscore the words: *small nations*. Indeed, what are the Jews if not a small nation, *the* small nation par excellence? The only one of all the small nations of all time that has survived empires and the devastating march of History.

But what is a small nation? I offer you my definition: the small nation is one whose very existence may be put in question at any moment; a small nation can disappear, and it knows it. A Frenchman, a Russian, or an Englishman is not used to asking questions about the very survival of his nation. His anthems speak only of grandeur and eternity. The Polish anthem, however, starts with the verse: "Poland has not yet perished . . ."

Central Europe as a family of small nations has its own vision of the world, a vision based on a deep distrust of History. History, that goddess of Hegel and Marx, that incarnation of reason that judges us and arbitrates our fate—that is the history of conquerors. The people of Central Europe are not conquerors. They cannot be separated from European history; they cannot exist outside it; but they represent the wrong side of this history; they are its victims and outsiders. It's this disabused view of history that is the source of their culture, of their wisdom, of the "nonserious spirit" that mocks grandeur and glory. "Never forget that only in opposing History as such can we resist the history of our own day." I would love to engrave this sentence by Witold Gombrowicz above the entry gate to Central Europe.

Thus it was in this region of small nations that have "not yet perished" that Europe's vulnerability was clearly visible before anywhere else. Actually, in our modern world where power has a tendency to become more and more concentrated in the hands of a few big countries, all European nations run the risk of becoming small nations and of sharing their fate. In this sense, the destiny of Central Europe anticipates the destiny of

Europe in general, and its culture assumes an enormous relevance.*

It's enough to read the greatest Central European novels: in Hermann Broch's *The Sleepwalkers*, History appears as a process of the gradual degradation of values; Robert Musil's *The Man without Qualities* paints a euphoric society that doesn't realize that tomorrow it will disappear; in Jaroslav Hašek's *The Good Soldier Schweik*, pretending to be an idiot becomes the last possible method for preserving one's freedom; the novelistic visions of Kafka speak to us of a world without memory, of a world that comes from historic time.†
All of this century's great Central European works of art, even up to our own day, can be understood

---

* The problem of Central European culture is examined in a very important periodical published by the University of Michigan: *Cross Currents: A Yearbook of Central European Culture.*

† With this constellation of Central European writers, among them Kafka, Hašek, Broch, and Musil, a new post-Proustian, post-Joycean aesthetic of the novel, it seems to me, arises in Europe. Broch is the one I personally care for the most. It's high time this Viennese novelist, one of the greatest of this century, was rediscovered.

as long meditations on the possible end of European humanity.

8.

Today, all of Central Europe has been subjugated by Russia with the exception of little Austria, which, more by chance than necessity, has retained its independence, but ripped out of its Central European setting, has lost most of its individual character and all its importance. The disappearance of the cultural home of Central Europe was certainly one of the greatest events of the century for all of Western civilization. So, I repeat my question: How could it possibly have gone unnoticed and unnamed?

The answer is simple: Europe hasn't noticed the disappearance of its cultural home because Europe no longer perceives its unity as a cultural unity.

In fact, what is European unity based on?

In the Middle Ages, it was based on a shared religion. In the modern era, in which the medieval God has been changed into a *Deus absconditus*, religion bowed out, giving way to culture, which became the expression of the supreme values by which European humanity understood itself, defined itself, identified itself as European.

Now it seems that another change is taking place in our century, as important as the one that divided the Middle Ages from the modern era. Just as God long ago gave way to culture, culture in turn is giving way.

But to what and to whom? What realm of supreme values will be capable of uniting Europe? Technical feats? The marketplace? The mass media? Will the great poet be replaced by the great journalist?* Or by politics? But by which politics? The Right or the Left? Is there a discernible shared ideal that still exists above the Manichaeanism of the Left and the Right that is as stupid as it is insurmountable? Will it be the principle of tolerance, respect for the beliefs and ideas of other people? But

---

* If journalism at one time seemed to be an appendix to culture, today, by contrast, culture finds itself at the mercy of journalism; it is part of a world dominated by journalism. The mass media decide who will be known and to what degree and according to which interpretation. The writer no longer addresses the public directly; he must communicate with it through the semitransparent barrier of the mass media.

won't this tolerance become empty and useless if it no longer protects a rich creativity or a strong set of ideas? Or should we understand the abdication of culture as a sort of deliverance, to which we should ecstatically abandon ourselves? Or will the *Deus absconditus* return to fill the empty space and reveal himself? I don't know, I know nothing about it. I think I know only that culture has bowed out.

9.

Franz Werfel spent the first third of his life in Prague, the second third in Vienna, and the last third as an emigrant, first in France, then in America—there you have a typically Central European biography. In 1937 he was in Paris with his wife, the famous Alma, Mahler's widow; he'd been invited there by the International Committee on Intellectual Cooperation within the League of Nations to a conference on "The Future of Literature." During the conference Werfel took a stand against not only Hitlerism but the totalitarian threat in general, the ideological and journalistic mindlessness of the times that was on the verge of destroying culture. He ended his speech with a proposal that he thought might arrest this demonic process: to found a World Academy of Poets and Thinkers (Weltakademie der Dichter und Denker). In no circumstance should the members be named by their states. The selection of members should be dependent only on the value of their work. The number of members, made up of the greatest writers in the world, should be between twenty-four and forty. The task of this academy, free of politics and propaganda, would be to "confront the politicization and barbarization of the world."

Not only was this proposal rejected, it was openly ridiculed. Of course, it was naive. Terribly naive. In a world absolutely politicized, in which artists and thinkers were already irremediably "committed," already politically *engagé*, how could such an independent academy possibly be created? Wouldn't it have the rather comic aspect of an assembly of noble souls?

However, this naive proposal strikes me as moving, because it reveals the desperate need to find once again a moral authority in a world stripped of values. It reveals the anguished desire to hear the inaudible voice of culture, the voice of Dichter und Denker.*

This story is mixed up in my mind with the memory of a morning when the police, after making a mess of the apartment of one of my friends, a famous Czech philosopher, confiscated a thousand pages of his philosophic manuscript. Shortly after, we were walking through the streets of Prague. We walked down from Hradčany Castle, where he lived, toward the peninsula of Kampa; we crossed the Maneš Bridge. He was trying to make a joke

---

* Werfel's speech was not at all naive and it has not lost its relevance. It reminds me of another speech, one that Robert Musil read in 1935 to the International Congress for the Defense of Culture in Paris. Like Werfel, Musil saw a danger not only in fascism but also in communism. The defense of culture for him did not mean the commitment of culture to a political struggle (as everyone else thought at the time), but on the contrary it meant the protection of culture from the mindlessness of politicization. Both writers realized that in the modern world of technology and mass media, the prospects of culture were not bright. Musil's and Werfel's opinions were very coolly received in Paris. However, in all the political and cultural discussions I hear about me, I would have almost nothing to add to what they have said, and I feel, in such moments, very close to them—I feel in those moments, irreparably Central European.

of it all: How were the police going to decipher his philosophical lingo, which was rather hermetic? But no joke could soothe his anguish, could make up for the loss of ten years of work that this manuscript represented—for he did not have another copy.

We talked about the possibility of sending an open letter abroad in order to turn this confiscation into an international scandal. It was perfectly clear to us that he should address the letter not to an institution or a statesman but only to some figure above politics, someone who stood for an unquestionable moral value, someone universally acknowledged in Europe. In other words, a great cultural figure. But who was this person?

Suddenly we understood that this figure did not exist. To be sure, there were great painters, playwrights, and musicians, but they no longer held a privileged place in society as moral authorities that Europe would acknowledge as its spiritual representatives. Culture no longer existed as a realm in which supreme values were enacted.

We walked toward the square in the old city near which I was then living, and we felt an immense loneliness, a void, the void in the European space from which culture was slowly withdrawing.*

10.

The last direct personal experience of the West that Central European countries remember is the period from 1918 to 1938. Their picture of the West, then, is of the West in the past, of a West in which culture had not yet entirely bowed out.

With this in mind, I want to stress a significant circumstance: the Central European revolts were not nourished by the newspapers, radio, or television—that

---

* At last, after hesitating, he sent the letter, after all—to Jean-Paul Sartre. Yes, he was the last great world cultural figure: on the other hand, he is the very person who, with his theory of "engagement," provided, in my opinion, the theoretical basis for the abdication of culture as an autonomous force, particular and irreducible. Despite what he might have been, he did respond promptly to my friend's letter with a statement published in *Le Monde*. Without this intervention, I doubt the police would have finally returned (nearly a year later) the manuscript of the philosopher. On the day Sartre was buried, the memory of my Prague friend came back to mind: now his letter would no longer find a recipient.

is, by the "media." They were prepared, shaped, realized by novels, poetry, theater, cinema, historiography,
literary reviews, popular comedy and cabaret, philosophical discussions—that is, by culture.* The mass
media—which, for the French and Americans, are indis-
tinguishable from whatever the West today is meant to
be—played no part in these revolts (since the press and
television were completely under state control).

That's why, when the Russians occupied Czechoslovakia, they did everything possible to destroy Czech

---

* By reviews, I mean periodicals (monthly, fortnightly, or weekly) run not by
journalists but by people of culture (writers, art critics, scholars, philosophers,
musicians); they deal with cultural questions and comment on social events from
the cultural point of view. In the nineteenth and twentieth centuries in Europe
and Russia, all the important intellectual movements formed around such reviews.
The German Romantic musicians clustered around the *Neue Zeitschrift für Musik*,
founded by Robert Schumann. Russian literature is unthinkable without such reviews as *Sovremennik* or *Viesy*, just as French literature depended on the *Nouvelle
Revue française* or *Les Temps modernes*. All Viennese cultural activity was concentrated around *Die Fackel*, directed by Karl Kraus. Gombrowicz's entire journal
was published in the Polish review *Kultura*, etc., etc. The disappearance of such
reviews from Western public life or the fact that they have become completely mar-
ginal is, in my opinion, a sign that "culture is bowing out."

culture.* This destruction had three meanings: first, it destroyed the center of the opposition; second, it undermined the identity of the nation, enabling it to be more easily swallowed up by Russian civilization; third, it put a violent end to the modern era, the era in which culture still represented the realization of supreme values.

This third consequence seems to me the most important. In effect, totalitarian Russian civilization is the radical negation of the modern West, the West created four centuries ago at the dawn of the modern era—the era founded on the authority of the thinking, doubting individual, and on an artistic creation that expressed his uniqueness. The Russian invasion has thrown Czechoslovakia into a "post-cultural" era and left it defenseless and naked before the Russian army and the omnipresent state television.

---

* Five hundred thousand people (especially intellectuals) were pushed out of their jobs. One hundred twenty thousand emigrated. About two hundred Czech and Slovak writers have been forbidden to publish. Their books have been banned from every public library and their names have been erased from history textbooks. One hundred forty-five Czech historians have been fired. From a single faculty of the university in Prague, fifty teachers were dismissed. (At the darkest moment of the Austro-Hungarian Empire, after the revolution of 1848, two Czech professors were driven out of the university—what a scandal at the time!) Every literary and cultural journal has been liquidated. The great Czech cinema, the great Czech theater no longer exist.

While still shaken by this triply tragic event that the invasion of Prague represented, I arrived in France and tried to explain to French friends the massacre of culture that had taken place after the invasion: "Try to imagine! All of the literary and cultural reviews were liquidated! Every one, without exception! That never happened before in Czech history, not even under the Nazi occupation during the war."

Then my friends would look at me indulgently with an embarrassment that I understood only later. When all the reviews in Czechoslovakia were liquidated, the entire nation knew it, and was in a state of anguish because of the immense impact of the event.* If all the reviews

---

* The weekly publication *Literární noviny* (Literary Journal), which had a circulation of three hundred thousand copies (in a land of ten million people), was produced by the Czech Writers' Congress. It was this publication that over the years led the way to the Prague Spring and was afterward a platform for it. It did not resemble such weeklies as *Time*, which have spread through Europe and America. No, it was truly literary: in it could be found long art chronicles, analyses of books. The articles devoted to history, sociology, and politics were not written by journalists but by writers, historians, and philosophers. I don't know of a single European weekly in our century that has played as important a historical role or played it as well. The circulation for Czech literary monthlies varied between ten thousand and forty thousand copies, and their level was remarkably high, in spite of censorship. In Poland, reviews have a comparable importance; today there are hundreds of underground journals there.

in France or England disappeared, no one would notice it, not even their editors. In Paris, even in a completely cultivated milieu, during dinner parties people discuss television programs, not reviews. For culture has already bowed out. Its disappearance, which we experienced in Prague as a catastrophe, a shock, a tragedy, is perceived in Paris as something banal and insignificant, scarcely visible, a nonevent.

11.

After the destruction of the Austrian Empire, Central Europe lost its ramparts. Didn't it lose its soul after Auschwitz, which swept the Jewish nation off its map? And after having been torn away from Europe in 1945, does Central Europe still exist?

Yes, its creativity and its revolts suggest that it has "not yet perished." But if to live means to exist in the eyes of those we love, then Central Europe no longer exists. More precisely: in the eyes of its beloved Europe,

Central Europe is just a part of the Soviet empire and nothing more, nothing more.

And why should this surprise us? By virtue of its political system, Central Europe is the East; by virtue of its cultural history, it is the West. But since Europe itself is in the process of losing its own cultural identity, it perceives in Central Europe nothing but a political regime; put another way, it sees in Central Europe only Eastern Europe.

Central Europe, therefore, should fight not only against its big oppressive neighbor but also against the subtle, relentless pressure of time, which is leaving the era of culture in its wake. That's why in Central European revolts there is something conservative, nearly anachronistic: they are desperately trying to restore the past, the past of culture, the past of the modern era. It is only in that period, only in a world that maintains a cultural dimension, that Central Europe can still defend its identity, still be seen for what it is.

The real tragedy for Central Europe, then, is not Russia but Europe: this Europe that represented a value so great that the director of the Hungarian News Agency was ready to die for it, and for which he did indeed die. Behind the Iron Curtain, he did not suspect that the times had changed and that in Europe itself Europe was no longer experienced as a value. He did not suspect that the sentence he was sending by telex beyond the borders of his flat country would seem outmoded and would not be understood.

—Translated from the French by Edmund White, published as "The Tragedy of Central Europe," in the *New York Review of Books* (April 26, 1984)

OTHER BOOKS BY MILAN KUNDERA

FICTION

Ignorance

Set in contemporary Prague, *Ignorance* takes up the complex and emotionally charged theme of exile and creates from it a literary masterpiece.

Identity

"A beguiling meditation on the illusions of self-image and desire."

—*Time Out New York*

"A fervent and compelling romance, a moving fable about the anxieties of love and separateness."

—*Baltimore Sun*

Slowness

"Irresistible.... An ode to sensuous leisure."

—*Mirabella*

"Audacity, wit, and sheer brilliance."

—*New York Times Book Review*

Immortality

From a woman's casual gesture to her swimming instructor springs a novel of the imagination that both embodies and articulates the great themes of existence.

"Ingenious, witty, provocative, and formidably intelligent, both a pleasure and a challenge to the reader."

—*Washington Post Book World*

The Unbearable Lightness of Being

"Mr. Kundera's novel composed in the spirit of the late quartets of Beethoven is concerned with the opposing elements of freedom and necessity among a quartet of entangled lovers."

—*New Yorker*

The Book of Laughter and Forgetting

"*The Book of Laughter and Forgetting* calls itself a novel, although it is part fairy tale, part literary criticism, part political tract, part musicology, and part autobiography. It can call itself whatever it wants to, because the whole is genius."

—*New York Times*

Farewell Waltz

Farewell Waltz poses the most serious questions with a blasphemous lightness that makes us see that the modern world has deprived us even of the right to tragedy.

"*Farewell Waltz* shocks. Black humor. Farcical ferocity."

—*Le Point* (Paris)

Life Is Elsewhere

"A remarkable portrait of an artist as(Paris) a young man."

—*Newsweek*

"A sly and merciless lampoon of revolutionary romanticism."

—*Time*

Laughable Loves

"Kundera takes some of Freud's most cherished complexes and irreverently whirls them about in acts of legerdemain that capture our darkest, deepest human passions. . . . Complex, full of mockeries and paradoxes."

—*Cleveland Plain Dealer*

The Joke

A student's innocent joke incurs hard punishment in Stalinist Czechoslovakia.

"A thoughtful, intricate, ambivalent novel."

—John Updike

The Festival of Insignificance

"There is a timeless quality to his philosophy about the importance of laughter. . . . Kundera is still the powerful and incisive writer he always was."

—*New York Times Book Review*

NONFICTION

The Curtain

A brilliant, delightful exploration of the novel—its history and its art—from one of the genre's most distinguished practitioners.

Testaments Betrayed

"A fascinating idiosyncratic meditation on the moral necessity of preserving the artist's work from destructive appraisal. . . . One reads this book to come in contact with one of the most stimulating minds of our era."

—*Boston Globe*

The Art of the Novel

"Every novelist's work contains an implicit vision of the history of the novel, an idea of what the novel is. I have tried to express the idea of the novel that is inherent in my own novels."

—Milan Kundera

Encounter

"Cultivated, worldly, charming, and spirited. . . . Kundera's values are sane and humane; his impulses generous; his taste, overall, unimpeachable."

—Phillip Lopate, *San Francisco Chronicle*

"I can't imagine reading this book without being challenged and instructed, amused, amazed and aroused, and ultimately delighted."

—John Simon, *New York Times Book Review*

THEATER

Jacques and His Master

Kundera's three-act stage adaptation of Diderot's eighteenth-century philosophical novel *Jacques le fataliste*.

The Franco-Czech novelist MILAN KUNDERA was born in Brno and has lived in France, his second homeland, since 1975. He is the author of the novels *The Joke*, *Life Is Elsewhere*, *Farewell Waltz*, *The Book of Laughter and Forgetting*, *The Unbearable Lightness of Being*, and *Immortality*, and the short story collection *Laughable Loves*—all originally in Czech. His more recent novels, *Slowness*, *Identity*, *Ignorance*, and *The Festival of Insignificance*, as well as his nonfiction works, *The Art of the Novel*, *Testaments Betrayed*, *The Curtain*, and *Encounter*, were originally written in French.